The Vineyard Discipleship Guides
Volume 1

Experience and Worship God
Partner with the Holy Spirit

Robert E. Logan with Charles R. Ridley

2nd edition

vineyard

vineyard discipleship guides

Published by Logan Leadership

Visit us at **http://loganleadership.com**

Unless otherwise indicated, all Scripture quotations are taken from the Holy Bible, New Living Translation, copyright © 1996, 2004, 2007, 2013 by Tyndale House Foundation. Used by permission of Tyndale House Publishers, Inc., Carol Stream, Illinois 60188. All rights reserved.

Scriptures noted (NIV) are taken from the Holy Bible, New International Version ®, NIV®. Copyright © 1973, 1978, 1984, 2011 by Biblica, Inc. ™ Used by permission of Zondervan. All rights reserved worldwide. www.zondervan.com The "NIV" and "New International Version" are trademarks registered in the United States Patent and Trademark Office by Biblica, Inc. ™

Quotes from Vineyard pastors and practitioners featured in "From the Vineyard" used by permission, Vineyard Resources, Vineyard Distinctives Series, 2016.

Copyright © 2017 Robert E. Logan. All rights reserved. 2nd Edition

ISBN: 978-1-944955-34-2

Printed in the United States of America

vineyard discipleship guides

Acknowledgements

Multiply Vineyard—Michael Gatlin and his team—initially helped with the contextualizing of our tree of discipleship to the Vineyard. We produced the first edition.

Then for more extended use with Vineyard internationally, Vineyard Missions—Mark Fields and his team—did a thorough assessment of discipleship needs and provided valuable feedback, resulting in this second edition.

Kande Milano contributed to the introduction and quotations from Vineyard leaders throughout, helping to adapt the material for the Vineyard Movement.

Tara Miller's exceptional writing skills brought our thoughts and ideas to life in the original version. Above all others, she made this book possible. Over many years, her creative collaboration has made it possible to give written resources to the Church so that people can discover and live out their God-given purpose.

vineyard discipleship guides

© 2017 Robert E. Logan

Contents

Discipleship in the Vineyard — 1

Experience and Worship God — 7

Growing in Experiencing and Worshipping God — 9

I. Actively living out and embracing the Kingdom of God — 13

II. Seeking to know God more deeply — 19

III. Reflecting on and applying scripture in your everyday life — 25

IV. Experiencing authentic interactive dialogue with God — 31

V. Worshipping with your whole life — 35

Partner with the Holy Spirit — 39

Growing in Partnering with the Holy Spirit — 41

I. Increasing ability to hear and discern God's voice — 45

II. Discerning where God is working and actively participating with him — 51

III. Checking what you're hearing with scripture and your Kingdom community — 55

IV. Risking action in steps of faith and service — 59

V. Discovering your giftedness and calling — 65

VI. Practicing spiritual disciplines in a way that increases our sensitivity and surrender to the Holy Spirit — 69

What's next? — 73

About the Authors — 77

About Logan Leadership — 77

vineyard discipleship guides

© 2017 Robert E. Logan

Introduction

Discipleship in the Vineyard

Love God. Love People.

Jesus said the greatest thing any of us can do is to love God with all of who we are and to love others as well as we love ourselves (Matthew 22:36). He taught that this kind of love is about more than **feeling differently;** it is also about **thinking and acting differently**. So when we say yes to becoming a follower, or disciple, of Jesus, we commit to expanding our capacity to love like he did. We do as Jesus did, listen to what he said, love who he loved and obey his teaching.

In the Vineyard, we affirm our commitment to "love God and love others" when we say we **embrace the Kingdom** and **engage the world**. With these words, we acknowledge what our "yes" to the good news of Jesus means. It is a personal response to Our Father's invitation into restored relationship with him. But it is also a response to the challenge of accepting God's Kingdom rule and reign, of making his mission our own. As we increasingly devote ourselves to him, we cannot help but pray with our Lord to see his Kingdom come in all its fullness, on earth as it is in heaven (Matthew 6:9-14). Both our relationships with and responsibilities to God and people are changed with our simple, faith-filled "yes."

Jesus modeled this way of life. Secure in his identity as beloved of God, he poured out that love to the world. Jesus came to earth fundamentally as a rescuer of people. He lovingly urged people to stop trying to manage life on their own terms, to turn toward him and believe his message: **the Kingdom of God is near!** (Mark 1:15-16) Love was and still is his mission, as he said:

> *"The Spirit of the Lord is upon me, for he has anointed me to bring Good News to the poor. He has sent me to proclaim that captives will be released, that the blind will see, that the oppressed will be set free, and that the time of the Lord's favor has come." (Luke 4:18–19)*

God continues to call each of us into this mission with Jesus. To be disciples who, like him, yearn to be with the Father and join in what we see him doing. This is foundational to the Vineyard. We are humble enough to know we change very little without him—bold enough to believe we can change the world with him.

vineyard discipleship guides

"So Jesus explained, 'I tell you the truth, the Son can do nothing by himself. He does only what he sees the Father doing. Whatever the Father does, the Son also does. For the Father loves the Son and shows him everything he is doing. In fact, the Father will show him how to do even greater works than healing this man. Then you will truly be astonished. For just as the Father gives life to those he raises from the dead, so the Son gives life to anyone he wants.'" (John 5:19-21)

What an adventure to be like Jesus, joining him in bringing life and hope to the world. But how?

Making it Personal

Before we can be ready to respond to God's call, we start by acknowledging where we are now. We are each on a spiritual journey: for truth, for purpose and relationship, for figuring out life. No matter where you are on yours, we are glad you are with us. The Vineyard is a safe place full of people with questions, just like you. Some of us have already decided to follow Jesus, while others haven't. None of us have everything figured out, but we do know a few things. First, we need to learn who God says he is. Second, we need to talk about what we're learning with others. And finally, at some point, we need to do something about it. Specifically, we:

- **Talk to God.** That's all prayer is. Pour your heart out. You don't need religious language. Just start talking. What should you say? Well, ask questions if you have them. And consider what you would say to someone who saved your life, who calls you His friend, and His child? Start by thanking Him.

- **Read the Bible.** Check to see if the Jesus you read about is any different from the Jesus you thought you knew. He wasn't just a nice guy who taught nice things. He was also a revolutionary. Don't worry about where to start or things you don't understand right away. Just read a little every day and ask a lot of questions as you go – both of God, and of other people around you.

- **Join with others.** The Holy Spirit meets us in unique ways when we gather together. Singing songs of worship reminds us of who and what is most important. Being taught from the scriptures provides a solid foundation and practical tools for daily life. Gathering with a few others to study offers a place to ask questions, support one another, and reflect on who God is. We need to learn from those who are further along in the faith than we are, and we need to be that person for others.

- **Take action.** We can only be on a journey if we are moving. Growth happens when we act on what we hear and have experienced. We also demonstrate our love for God and others through acts of service, obedience and devotion. Again and again we ask "What do I hear the Father saying? And what am I going to do about it?"

vineyard discipleship guides

from the vineyard

"The Meat is in the Street"

Vineyard founder John Wimber sometimes found himself at a loss for what to say to those who said they wanted to become mature disciples by delving into the deeper "meat" of the Word. During one such time, he sensed the Holy Spirit saying, "John, the 'meat' is in the street." He understood the Lord to be telling him that "discipleship is not so much what one knows as it is what one does with what one knows."

– **As told in Kingdom Evangelism booklet, Vineyard Ministries International**

How we learn God's truth, grow alongside others, and act upon our beliefs may change over time, but our need for these practices doesn't. Scripture encourages us this way:

> "Let us think of ways to motivate one another to acts of love and good works. And let us not neglect our meeting together, as some people do, but encourage one another, especially now that the day of his return is drawing near." (Hebrews 10:24-25)

Guides for the Journey

We have written these discipleship guides to help you get started practicing Hebrews 10:24-25. Consider them a travel guide in your journey. To begin, find three or four others to meet with regularly. Then use the guides to create a predictable pattern for what happens each time you gather. Ask one another the suggested questions. Wait and listen to responses from the heart. Encourage, challenge and affirm one another. Go at your own pace. Just be sure to allow enough time between your gatherings to practice these new behaviors.

As you go, remember to be kind to yourself and your fellow travelers. We each come to this process just as we are, delighted to find ourselves accepted and loved. We also learn that God loves us too much to let us stay as we are. Discipleship is not something we ever finish in this lifetime. And we don't expect to be perfect. Once we come to faith in Jesus, however, we must be willing to submit our whole life to God. Jesus expected such whole-hearted devotion:

vineyard discipleship guides

But don't begin until you count the cost. For who would begin construction of a building without first calculating the cost to see if there is enough money to finish it? Otherwise, you might complete only the foundation before running out of money, and then everyone would laugh at you. They would say, 'There's the person who started that building and couldn't afford to finish it!" (Luke 14:28-30)

True discipleship embraces ongoing growth in all areas of life. We cannot be content with looking like Christ in some ways while remaining unchanged in others. A disciple when fully trained is like his or her teacher, Jesus (Luke 6:40). We continue to grow in knowing, being and doing. We are baptized, become fishers of people, obey and make disciples. We are transformed and transforming. We move toward whole-hearted commitment to God and his Kingdom. The process of discipleship is life-on-life, face-to-face, and hand-in-hand.

So What's Next?

As Jesus came to be among us, we see him living and loving in ways that can be categorized into eight sets of behaviors, which we have diagrammed on a tree. Each of these eight areas has a corresponding discipleship guide. Examine the Discipleship Tree to see how all the pieces fit together.

© 2017 Robert E. Logan

vineyard discipleship guides

Experience and Worship God, at the root, focuses on the way we interact and talk with God, the way our awareness of his presence grows, and how we personally worship him. This root is necessary for all of the other areas, as they flow out of our experience of God. For this reason, we recommend everyone start with this study.

Next, you see the trunk of the tree, **Partner with the Holy Spirit**. This guide is about actively listening to the Holy Spirit and acting on what you hear. It connects our experience of God to the ways in which we respond to him.

Once you have worked through these two foundational guides with your group, choose whichever of the remaining six guides you like. They each explore a dimension of discipleship that flows from the foundation of knowing God and staying in tune with him. From that place of connection, you can trust the Holy Spirit to lead you.

Throughout each of the guides, you will encounter special notes labeled "From the Vineyard," like the one earlier in this section. The core material in the guides represents what you might think of as the "main and plain" of what following Jesus looks like. Consider these additional notes an offering of insight from some of your more experienced Vineyard friends.

There is always a next step in the journey of faith. What's yours?

vineyard discipleship guides

Experience and Worship God

Engage consistently with God, intentionally deepening your relationship and allowing your experience of his presence to fuel your life in the Kingdom

vineyard discipleship guides

© 2017 Robert E. Logan

Growing in Experiencing and Worshipping God

The Vineyard Discipleship Guides are organized according to the tree diagram below; examine it to see how all of the pieces fit together.

Experience and Worship God, at the root of the tree, focuses on the way we interact and dialogue with God, the way we become increasingly aware of his presence, and how we continue to worship him personally. This root is necessary for all of the other areas, as they flow out of our experience of God.

vineyard discipleship guides

from the vineyard

> "We in the Vineyard have, from the very outset of our ministry, made worship our highest priority, believing that it is God's desire that we become, first, worshippers of God."
>
> – **John Wimber**

Worship means both being invited into a deeper relationship with God, as well as being challenged toward greater involvement in his Kingdom mission. We are to be intentionally and intimately engaging with God in such a way that we open ourselves to a deeper relationship with him and his Kingdom. We are to use our minds, our bodies, our souls, and our emotions to love him.

> *"He answered, '"Love the Lord your God with all your heart and with all your soul and with all your strength and with all your mind'; and, 'Love your neighbor as yourself.'"* –Luke 10:27 (NIV)

> *"... true worshipers will worship the Father in the Spirit and in truth, for they are the kind of worshipers the Father seeks."* –John 4:23 (NIV)

> *"Therefore, I urge you, brothers and sisters, in view of God's mercy, to offer your bodies as a living sacrifice, holy and pleasing to God—this is your true and proper worship."* –Romans 12:1 (NIV)

We can engage with God through all of our senses and in many different ways: through music, through prayer, through scripture, through the natural world. The methods of experiencing God's presence, the ways that we can worship him are infinite. The following five-part journey covers these five essential expressions of experiencing and worshipping God:

- **Actively living out and embracing the Kingdom of God**
- **Seeking to know God more deeply**
- **Reflecting on and applying scripture in your everyday life**
- **Experiencing authentic, interactive dialogue with God**
- **Worshipping with your whole life**

Experience and Worship God

Group structure

Meet together with a group of three or four to talk through each of these expressions. Choose people who will be faithful and supportive, yet not afraid to challenge you toward growth. These should be people you trust to speak into your life.

When you meet, open by following up on your most recent time together. Ask each other these questions:

- **What are you especially thankful for since we last gathered?**
- **What are your current challenges?**
- **Is there some way we can help?**
- **With whom did you share your learnings from our last time together?**
- **How did it go with your action items from last time?**

Remember how John Wimber used to say: "Everyone gets to play." That means everyone has the opportunity to minister to one another, pray for one another, and listen to discern God's voice.

Then dive into the material for this week. Read scripture passages and ask one another the questions. Wait for and listen to responses from the heart. Encourage, challenge, and affirm one another.

Allow ministry time and prayer at the end of your gathering. There is great value in doing life together and consistently praying for one another and ministering together.

Go at your own pace: you can do one a week or one a month, whatever pace works best for you. Be sure to allow enough time to live into these behaviors, because next time you meet you'll begin by asking each other the same follow up questions about your action items.

vineyard discipleship guides

I. Actively living out and embracing the Kingdom of God

Key question: How are you actively living out and embracing the Kingdom of God?

Sometimes we feel a sense of God's presence on an emotional level and sometimes we don't. We know he is always there, regardless of how we feel. How can we go about living out our faith even when he feels far away from us? How can we attune ourselves to the reality of his Kingdom?

from the vineyard

> "We are a people who have been awakened to the reality that God is not nearly as far away as we once thought. He's near - he is always near! And it is his nearness that shapes everything we do and everything we are."
>
> – **Adam Russell**

The presence of God and his Kingdom is what sustains and nourishes us when we have trouble or when difficult journeys are ahead of us. Much as Jesus gave us his body and blood at the last supper, we continue to need that nourishment from the Spirit of God to sustain us and help us move forward.

Sometimes we sense his love and presence in the big things—the major changes and challenges in our lives—and sometimes we sense his love and presence in the small things—a gentle breeze or the sun on our face. Our goal in living out and embracing the Kingdom of God is not manufacturing emotion, but getting in touch with how God is already speaking to us and then recognizing his presence in our lives. From that foundation we live.

vineyard discipleship guides

Meditation

Bede Griffiths, a Benedictine monk, details something he experienced as a boy. He was walking in the evening when he was suddenly dazzled by the beautiful song of a flock of birds. The beauty of their singing seemed to awaken senses he'd never used before. In an instant the world seemed magically transformed, and everything in it seemed to burst with what he calls a "kind of sacramental character. I remember now the feeling of awe which came over me," he wrote, "I felt inclined to kneel on the ground... and I hardly dared to look on the face of the sky, because it seemed as though it was but a veil before the face of God."

When have you experienced something like this? Take time to re-imagine that time in your mind, re-creating the sensory experience.

This week read and reflect daily on the scripture below. Open a natural flow of conversational prayer with the Holy Spirit as you meditate on the scriptures, inviting him to reveal himself to you. Then gather with those who journey alongside you and interact over the discipleship questions.

1 Kings 19:3-18

> *Elijah was afraid and fled for his life. He went to Beersheba, a town in Judah, and he left his servant there. 4 Then he went on alone into the wilderness, traveling all day. He sat down under a solitary broom tree and prayed that he might die. "I have had enough, Lord," he said. "Take my life, for I am no better than my ancestors who have already died."*
>
> *5 Then he lay down and slept under the broom tree. But as he was sleeping, an angel touched him and told him, "Get up and eat!" 6 He looked around and there beside his head was some bread baked on hot stones and a jar of water! So he ate and drank and lay down again.*
>
> *7 Then the angel of the Lord came again and touched him and said, "Get up and eat some more, or the journey ahead will be too much for you."*
>
> *8 So he got up and ate and drank, and the food gave him enough strength to travel forty days and forty nights to Mount Sinai, the mountain of God. 9 There he came to a cave, where he spent the night.*
>
> *But the Lord said to him, "What are you doing here, Elijah?"*
>
> *10 Elijah replied, "I have zealously served the Lord God Almighty. But the people of Israel have broken their covenant with you, torn down your altars, and killed every one of your prophets. I am the only one left, and now they are trying to kill me, too."*

Experience and Worship God

11 "Go out and stand before me on the mountain," the Lord told him. And as Elijah stood there, the Lord passed by, and a mighty windstorm hit the mountain. It was such a terrible blast that the rocks were torn loose, but the Lord was not in the wind. After the wind there was an earthquake, but the Lord was not in the earthquake. 12 And after the earthquake there was a fire, but the Lord was not in the fire. And after the fire there was the sound of a gentle whisper. 13 When Elijah heard it, he wrapped his face in his cloak and went out and stood at the entrance of the cave.

And a voice said, "What are you doing here, Elijah?"

14 He replied again, "I have zealously served the Lord God Almighty. But the people of Israel have broken their covenant with you, torn down your altars, and killed every one of your prophets. I am the only one left, and now they are trying to kill me, too."

15 Then the Lord told him, "Go back the same way you came, and travel to the wilderness of Damascus. When you arrive there, anoint Hazael to be king of Aram. 16 Then anoint Jehu grandson of Nimshi to be king of Israel, and anoint Elisha son of Shaphat from the town of Abel-meholah to replace you as my prophet. 17 Anyone who escapes from Hazael will be killed by Jehu, and those who escape Jehu will be killed by Elisha! 18 Yet I will preserve 7,000 others in Israel who have never bowed down to Baal or kissed him!"

Discipleship questions

- When are you most aware of God's presence and love?

- When are you most able to live out of that presence and love?

- In what ways are you embracing his Kingdom?

- Under what circumstances are you most likely to seek out his presence?

- How does God manifest his love for you?

- How might you be able to best grow in actively living out and embracing the Kingdom of God?

- What changes might be beneficial to you?

Action step questions

- **In light of our discussion, what do you hear God asking of you?**

- **How will you obey his prompting?**

- **When will you do it?**

- **Who will help you?**

- **With whom will you share what you have learned before we meet again?**

II. Seeking to know God more deeply

Key question: In what ways are you seeking to know God more deeply?

God has placed a hunger within us to know him. We can try many different ways to dampen, ignore, or redirect that hunger, but it remains buried within us. It's part of the natural blueprint of who we are. God made us not only as feeling people but thinking people. We wonder, we question, we evaluate. Our minds hunger to know God and to understand him. Toward that end, we engage with him in much the same way we would engage with another person: we seek to know them and to understand them. We ask questions, we listen, we observe.

from the vineyard

"For the Vineyard family of churches, experiencing God in the midst of personal or corporate worship has always been one of our core values. We are, at our very foundation, a people who find their greatest identity, strength, and joy in the presence of God."

– **Phil Strout**

This week read and reflect daily on the scripture below. Open a natural flow of conversational prayer with the Holy Spirit as you meditate on the scriptures, inviting him to reveal himself to you. Then gather with those who journey alongside you and interact over the discipleship questions.

Psalm 42:1-2

> *As the deer longs for streams of water,*
> *so I long for you, O God.*
>
> *2 I thirst for God, the living God.*
> *When can I go and stand before him?*

2 Peter 3:18

> *Rather, you must grow in the grace and knowledge of our Lord and Savior Jesus Christ.*

Colossians 2:1-9

I want you to know how much I have agonized for you and for the church at Laodicea, and for many other believers who have never met me personally. 2 I want them to be encouraged and knit together by strong ties of love. I want them to have complete confidence that they understand God's mysterious plan, which is Christ himself. 3 In him lie hidden all the treasures of wisdom and knowledge.

4 I am telling you this so no one will deceive you with well-crafted arguments. 5 For though I am far away from you, my heart is with you. And I rejoice that you are living as you should and that your faith in Christ is strong.

6 And now, just as you accepted Christ Jesus as your Lord, you must continue to follow him. 7 Let your roots grow down into him, and let your lives be built on him. Then your faith will grow strong in the truth you were taught, and you will overflow with thankfulness.

8 Don't let anyone capture you with empty philosophies and high-sounding nonsense that come from human thinking and from the spiritual powers of this world, rather than from Christ. 9 For in Christ lives all the fullness of God in a human body.

Experience and Worship God

 Discipleship questions:

- In what ways are you seeking to know God more deeply?

- What have you learned about God lately?

- How are you growing in knowledge? How are you growing in grace?

- Which qualities of God's character are you deepening your understanding of?

- How do the Father, the Son and the Holy Spirit each help you in your understanding of God?

- How are you experiencing the mystery of God?

- What effect does the knowledge of God have on your daily life?

- What qualities in your life has your deepening understanding of God resulted in? (e.g. hope, faith)

- In what ways might you continue to grow in this area?

- What changes might be beneficial to you?

ask God your questions

God is unafraid of our questions and unshaken by our doubts. He is not threatened or diminished in any way by our inquiries. Take some time to write out your questions to God. What do you wonder? What do you want to know? What really matters to you?

Experience and Worship God

 Action step questions:

- **In light of our discussion, what do you hear God asking of you?**

- **How will you obey his prompting?**

- **When will you do it?**

- **Who will help you?**

- **With whom will you share what you have learned before we meet again?**

vineyard discipleship guides

© 2017 Robert E. Logan

III. Reflecting on and applying scripture in your everyday life

Key question: How are you reflecting on and applying scripture in your everyday life?

One of the greatest gifts God has given us is his Word, the scriptures. Through the scriptures, we learn more about who God is, what he has done for us, and how we can serve him. All the genres are there: history, poetry, stories, songs, plays, philosophy, apocalyptic literature. It's left to us to figure out how we can best delve into this treasure trove of riches God has given to us.

Different strategies and approaches work best for different people. Some prefer to meditate for a long period of time on a short passage of scripture—reading and rereading it to fully experience the passage. Others prefer to read broad, large portions of scripture to see the overall narrative arc and context of the Word of God. Some don't prefer reading at all, but listening. After all, that's how most people have experienced scripture throughout history: they had it read to them. Memorization is another helpful approach for many in that it allows internalization of the ideas to a greater degree.

One important point is to find out what works for you and do it. As you faithfully interact with scripture, you will meet God there, as the Spirit speaks to you through his Word. The second point is to not walk away from what you are learning, but apply it in your everyday life. Understanding without application is useless.

> **from the vineyard**
>
> "It's not just about being biblically literate, we must also become biblically obedient."
>
> – **John Wimber**

This week read and reflect daily on the scripture below. Open a natural flow of conversational prayer with the Holy Spirit as you meditate on the scriptures, inviting him to reveal himself to you. Then gather with those who journey alongside you and interact over the discipleship questions.

2 Timothy 3:16-17

All Scripture is inspired by God and is useful to teach us what is true and to make us realize what is wrong in our lives. It corrects us when we are wrong and teaches us to do what is right. 17 God uses it to prepare and equip his people to do every good work.

Psalm 1:1-3

*Oh, the joys of those who do not
  follow the advice of the wicked,
  or stand around with sinners,
  or join in with mockers.*

*2 But they delight in the law of the Lord,
  meditating on it day and night.*

*3 They are like trees planted along the riverbank,
  bearing fruit each season.
  Their leaves never wither,
  and they prosper in all they do.*

Psalm 119:9-16

*How can a young person stay pure?
  By obeying your word.*

*10 I have tried hard to find you—
  don't let me wander from your commands.*

*11 I have hidden your word in my heart,
  that I might not sin against you.*

*12 I praise you, O Lord;
  teach me your decrees.*

*13 I have recited aloud
  all the regulations you have given us.*

*14 I have rejoiced in your laws
  as much as in riches.*

*15 I will study your commandments
  and reflect on your ways.*

*16 I will delight in your decrees
  and not forget your word.*

Experience and Worship God

 Discipleship questions:

- How do you best interact with scripture?

- What approaches have you tried?

- In which ways do you experience two-way communication as you interact with scripture?

- Which sections of scripture are you most drawn to and why?

- How do you structure your time in scripture? (e.g. a few minutes each day? a larger portion of time once a week?)

- Describe a typical time spent interacting with scripture.

- When is the last time you made a change in your life based on something you learned in scripture? Describe that time.

vineyard discipleship guides

- **When was one time God spoke to you clearly through the scriptures? How did you respond?**

- **In what ways do you see yourself needing to grow in this area?**

- **What changes might be beneficial to you?**

conduct a survey

Interview others within the body of Christ about the ways they engage with scripture. Ask them about practices such as mediating on a particular verse, reading large quantities of scripture, memorizing passages, and listening to scripture read aloud. What practices are most meaningful to them? When have they most powerfully experienced God through scripture?

Action step questions:

- **In light of our discussion, what do you hear God asking of you?**

- **How will you obey his prompting?**

- **When will you do it?**

- **Who will help you?**

- **With whom will you share what you have learned before we meet again?**

vineyard discipleship guides

IV. Experiencing authentic interactive dialogue with God

Key question: How do you dialogue authentically and interactively with God?

Our experience of God was never intended to be rote: a dutiful prayer asking for things and a routine reading of a chapter of the Bible a day. One of the revolutionary things about Jesus coming to earth incarnate was the communication that this whole worship thing is a relationship. With the death of Jesus, the curtain of the temple was ripped from top to bottom (that's the curtain separating the holy of holies from humanity). That barrier has been broken, and we can enter the presence of God through faith in Jesus, our mediator.

What we have now is not simply a set of duties or a book of rules. It's a real live relationship with another person. What do we do in relationships? We talk. We listen. We laugh. We spend time in each other's presence… sometimes without any agenda at all other than enjoying one another.

Now in the context of a relationship with the creator and Lord of the universe, how does that differ? Certainly, we worship. He is far above us. Yet he is also near, and we had best not remove the relational element. That forms the very core of our worship of God.

As Brother Lawrence wrote, "The time of business does not differ with me from the time of prayer; and in the noise and clatter of my kitchen, while several persons are at the same time calling for different things, I possess God in as great tranquility as if I were on my knees."

This week read and reflect daily on the following scripture. Open a natural flow of conversational prayer with the Holy Spirit as you meditate on the scriptures, inviting him to reveal himself to you. Then gather with those who journey alongside you and interact over the discipleship questions.

vineyard discipleship guides

Matthew 27:45-52

At noon, darkness fell across the whole land until three o'clock. 46 At about three o'clock, Jesus called out with a loud voice, "Eli, Eli, lema sabachthani?" which means "My God, my God, why have you abandoned me?"

47 Some of the bystanders misunderstood and thought he was calling for the prophet Elijah. 48 One of them ran and filled a sponge with sour wine, holding it up to him on a reed stick so he could drink. 49 But the rest said, "Wait! Let's see whether Elijah comes to save him."

50 Then Jesus shouted out again, and he released his spirit. 51 At that moment the curtain in the sanctuary of the Temple was torn in two, from top to bottom. The earth shook, rocks split apart, 52 and tombs opened. The bodies of many godly men and women who had died were raised from the dead.

Isaiah 6:1-8

It was in the year King Uzziah died that I saw the Lord. He was sitting on a lofty throne, and the train of his robe filled the Temple. 2 Attending him were mighty seraphim, each having six wings. With two wings they covered their faces, with two they covered their feet, and with two they flew. 3 They were calling out to each other,
"Holy, holy, holy is the Lord of Heaven's Armies!
The whole earth is filled with his glory!"

4 Their voices shook the Temple to its foundations, and the entire building was filled with smoke.

5 Then I said, "It's all over! I am doomed, for I am a sinful man. I have filthy lips, and I live among a people with filthy lips. Yet I have seen the King, the Lord of Heaven's Armies."

6 Then one of the seraphim flew to me with a burning coal he had taken from the altar with a pair of tongs. 7 He touched my lips with it and said, "See, this coal has touched your lips. Now your guilt is removed, and your sins are forgiven."

8 Then I heard the Lord asking, "Whom should I send as a messenger to this people? Who will go for us?"
I said, "Here I am. Send me."

Discipleship questions:

- When have you processed your disappointment or anger with God?

- When have you experienced awe of God?

- What do you need to tell God that you have not already told him?

- In what ways could you further open yourself up to honest dialogue with God?

- What changes might be beneficial to you?

Action step questions:

- In light of our discussion, what do you hear God asking of you?

- How will you obey his prompting?

- When will you do it?

- Who will help you?

- With whom will you share what you have learned before we meet again?

V. Worshipping with your whole life

Key question: How are you actively worshipping with your whole life?

We are people designed to worship. If we do not worship God, we will worship something: success, material possessions, another person. How can we worship God in spirit and in truth as he wants to be worshipped? Interacting with him in a humble, intimate, self-disclosing manner—willing to rearrange our lives in any way he might direct.

When people hear the word "worship," they often think of a Sunday morning worship service—something corporate with a large group and singing. That can certainly be part of worship, but worship is much larger than that. We also worship with our time, talent and treasure.

In the Old Testament, God showed that all of life was to revolve around himself—he's the center—even in the way the Israelites were to set up camp in the times of the Exodus. In the coming of Jesus we see the lengths to which God will go to love and redeem our lives.

It's not a matter of "getting things right" in a Pharisaical approach to God, but a matter of approaching God in a manner of "spirit and in truth," in the way Jesus described it to the woman at the well. It's an entire lifestyle of worship. For each of us that will look different and varied, just as all of creation is varied. The heart and soul of the Christian life is learning to hear the voice of God and developing to courage to do what he tells us to do. That is a life of worship.

whole life worship

> To worship God fully, with your whole life, make a list of all the areas of your life that need to come into submission to him (e.g. your relationships, your money, your sexuality, your work life, etc.) What areas of your life are you currently keeping separate from your worship of God? How might you go about integrating those areas?

This week read and reflect daily on the scripture below. Open a natural flow of conversational prayer with the Holy Spirit as you meditate on the scriptures, inviting him to reveal himself to you. Then gather with those who journey alongside you and interact over the discipleship questions.

from the vineyard

> "Our journey is one of life, and our worship is a living sacrifice before a living God. That is a life of simple devotion to Christ."
>
> – David Ruis

John 4:19-24

"Sir," the woman said, "you must be a prophet. 20 So tell me, why is it that you Jews insist that Jerusalem is the only place of worship, while we Samaritans claim it is here at Mount Gerizim, where our ancestors worshiped?"
21 Jesus replied, "Believe me, dear woman, the time is coming when it will no longer matter whether you worship the Father on this mountain or in Jerusalem. 22 You Samaritans know very little about the one you worship, while we Jews know all about him, for salvation comes through the Jews. 23 But the time is coming—indeed it's here now—when true worshipers will worship the Father in spirit and in truth. The Father is looking for those who will worship him that way. 24 For God is Spirit, so those who worship him must worship in spirit and in truth."

Exodus 33:8-11

Whenever Moses went out to the Tent of Meeting, all the people would get up and stand in the entrances of their own tents. They would all watch Moses until he disappeared inside. 9 As he went into the tent, the pillar of cloud would come down and hover at its entrance while the Lord spoke with Moses. 10 When the people saw the cloud standing at the entrance of the tent, they would stand and bow down in front of their own tents. 11 Inside the Tent of Meeting, the Lord would speak to Moses face to face, as one speaks to a friend. Afterward Moses would return to the camp, but the young man who assisted him, Joshua son of Nun, would remain behind in the Tent of Meeting.

journal

What does whole life worship look like for you? Describe what you look like (where, when, doing what) when you are fully engaged with God in worship.

Discipleship questions:

- What is your understanding of "whole life worship"?

- How do you bring your whole self before God?

- What else does God want you to bring to the table that you've not yet brought?

- In what ways do you feel like you bring your true self before God? In what ways is that hard?

- How do you see God as you worship him?

Action step questions:

- In light of our discussion, what do you hear God asking of you?

- How will you obey his prompting?

- When will you do it?

- Who will help you?

- With whom will you share what you have learned before we meet again?

Partner with the Holy Spirit

Actively listening to the Holy Spirit and taking action according to what you are hearing

Growing in Partnering with the Holy Spirit

The Vineyard Discipleship Guides are organized according to the tree diagram below; examine it to see how all of the pieces fit together.

Partner with the Holy Spirit describes how we choose to respond to the work of God in our lives. It involves actively listening and then taking action according to what we are hearing. God is present and at work in the world, drawing us closer to him. How we decide to respond is up to us. Scripture advises us on this count:

"Since we are living by the Spirit, let us follow the Spirit's leading in every part of our lives." –Galatians 5:25

"Trust in the Lord with all your heart; do not depend on your own understanding. Seek his will in all you do, and he will show you which path to take." –Proverbs 3:5-6

"Do not merely listen to the word, and so deceive yourselves. Do what it says." – James 1:22 (NIV)

"Jesus gave them this answer: 'Very truly I tell you, the Son can do nothing by himself; he can do only what he sees his Father doing, because whatever the Father does the Son also does. For the Father loves the Son and shows him all he does. Yes, and he will show him even greater works than these, so that you will be amazed." – John 5:19-20 (NIV)

As God draws near to us through his scriptures, through other people, and through the Holy Spirit, what will we do? Will we run and hide, as Adam and Eve did in the garden? Will we step forward in faith even when we don't know what's next, as Abraham did? How will we open ourselves to hearing God's voice and discerning what he is calling us to do? The Partner with the Holy Spirit guide is designed to help us engage questions like these. The following six-part journey covers these essential expressions:

- **Increasing ability to hear and discern God's voice**
- **Discerning where God is working and actively participating with him**
- **Checking what you're hearing with scripture and your Kingdom community**
- **Risking action in steps of faith and service**
- **Discovering your giftedness and calling**
- **Practicing spiritual disciplines in a way that increases our sensitivity and surrender to the Holy Spirit**

Group structure

Meet together with a group of three or four to talk through each of these expressions. Choose people who will be faithful and supportive, yet not afraid to challenge you toward growth. These should be people you trust to speak into your life.

Partner with the Holy Spirit

When you meet, open by following up on your most recent time together. Ask each other these questions:

- **What are you especially thankful for since we last gathered?**
- **What are your current challenges?**
- **Is there some way we can help?**
- **With whom did you share your learnings from our last time together?**
- **How did it go with your action items from last time?**

Remember how John Wimber used to say: "Everyone gets to play." That means everyone has the opportunity to minister to one another, pray for one another, and listen to discern God's voice.

Then dive into the material for this week. Read scripture passages and ask one another the questions. Wait for and listen to responses from the heart. Encourage, challenge, and affirm one another.

Allow ministry time and prayer at the end of your gathering. There is great value in doing life together and consistently praying for one another and ministering together.

Go at your own pace: you can do one a week or one a month, whatever pace works best for you. Be sure to allow enough time to live into these behaviors, because next time you meet you'll begin by asking each other the same follow up questions about your action items.

I. Increasing ability to hear and discern God's voice

Key question: How are you opening yourself up to hearing and discerning God's voice?

We cannot live as we are called to live on our own. We are simply not capable of it. We need the power of the Holy Spirit. Only the Holy Spirit guiding us and speaking to us and empowering us will allow us to respond to what God is calling us to do. We are in a position of need.

How then can we open ourselves to the Holy Spirit? How can we listen for his voice? How can we receive his power? We need to come to God in prayer with a spirit of humility and supplication, recognizing that without the power of the Spirit, we cannot live out what God has called us toward. That power is how the early church was built and how the church continues to be built—through our receiving guidance and empowerment from the Spirit.

from the vineyard

> "'Come, Holy Spirit' is a direct, bold request for the Spirit to do the work the Father wants to do in us, and to be the fire that propels us out to do the work the Father wants to do through us."
>
> – Steve and Cindy Nicholson

When we hear the Spirit calling us to do something, we can respond in a prayer of confirmation: "Yes, Lord," and "Come, Holy Spirit." Then we need to step forward in faith and do it, relying on God to see it through. We can do all things through Christ, who strengths us (Philippians 4:13).

prayer

Ask God to fill you with his power and his Spirit. Ask him to guide you toward what he wants you to do. Ask him to give you a listening ear for his voice and a willing heart to obey it. Then wait in a posture of attentiveness.

vineyard discipleship guides

This week read and reflect daily on the scripture below. Open a natural flow of conversational prayer with the Holy Spirit as you meditate on the scriptures, inviting him to reveal himself to you. Then gather with those who journey alongside you and interact over the discipleship questions.

Luke 24:49

And now I will send the Holy Spirit, just as my Father promised. But stay here in the city until the Holy Spirit comes and fills you with power from heaven."

Acts 2:1-21

On the day of Pentecost all the believers were meeting together in one place. 2 Suddenly, there was a sound from heaven like the roaring of a mighty windstorm, and it filled the house where they were sitting. 3 Then, what looked like flames or tongues of fire appeared and settled on each of them. 4 And everyone present was filled with the Holy Spirit and began speaking in other languages, as the Holy Spirit gave them this ability.

5 At that time there were devout Jews from every nation living in Jerusalem. 6 When they heard the loud noise, everyone came running, and they were bewildered to hear their own languages being spoken by the believers.

7 They were completely amazed. "How can this be?" they exclaimed. "These people are all from Galilee, 8 and yet we hear them speaking in our own native languages! 9 Here we are—Parthians, Medes, Elamites, people from Mesopotamia, Judea, Cappadocia, Pontus, the province of Asia, 10 Phrygia, Pamphylia, Egypt, and the areas of Libya around Cyrene, visitors from Rome 11 (both Jews and converts to Judaism), Cretans, and Arabs. And we all hear these people speaking in our own languages about the wonderful things God has done!" 12 They stood there amazed and perplexed. "What can this mean?" they asked each other.

13 But others in the crowd ridiculed them, saying, "They're just drunk, that's all!"

14 Then Peter stepped forward with the eleven other apostles and shouted to the crowd, "Listen carefully, all of you, fellow Jews and residents of Jerusalem! Make no mistake about this. 15 These people are not drunk, as some of you are assuming. Nine o'clock in the morning is much too early for that. 16 No, what you see was predicted long ago by the prophet Joel:

17 'In the last days,' God says,
   'I will pour out my Spirit upon all people.
Your sons and daughters will prophesy.
   Your young men will see visions,
   and your old men will dream dreams.

Partner with the Holy Spirit

*18 In those days I will pour out my Spirit
even on my servants—men and women alike—
and they will prophesy.*

*19 And I will cause wonders in the heavens above
and signs on the earth below—
blood and fire and clouds of smoke.*

*20 The sun will become dark,
and the moon will turn blood red
before that great and glorious day of the Lord arrives.*

*21 But everyone who calls on the name of the Lord
will be saved.'*

vineyard discipleship guides

Discipleship questions:

- When have you been most aware of hearing God's voice?

- How are you relying on the Holy Spirit?

- How are you waiting for him?

- What are you hearing from the Holy Spirit? How are you listening?

- What do you really want God to empower you to do?

- How can you pray for one another as you wait to receive guidance and empowerment from the Spirit?

Action step questions:

- **In light of our discussion, what do you hear God asking of you?**

- **How will you obey his prompting?**

- **When will you do it?**

- **Who will help you?**

- **With whom will you share what you have learned before we meet again?**

vineyard discipleship guides

II. Discerning where God is working and actively participating with him

Key question: Where—and in whom—do you see God working? How can you join him in what he is doing?

One of the most powerful recognitions we can have as we respond to the leading of God is that he has already gone before us. We are not alone; he already sent his Holy Spirit to prepare the way. He calls us to be faithful, to do what we can with what we have, but the results of our faithfulness do not lie with us.

God is already at work in others long before we come on the scene. He chooses to use us and work through us. Part of our faithfulness is simply paying attention to what God is already doing and following his lead. In this way we are naturally supernatural.

from the vineyard

> "John [Wimber] wasn't interested in wowing the crowd. There was no hype, weirdness or manipulation. When he ministered, he was relaxed, comfortable, real. I was impressed with how he remained normal while worshipping and praying. John called it being 'naturally supernatural.'"
>
> – Mike Turrigiano

God is at work everywhere—all around us. Look around you. Where can you see him at work? What evidence has he left behind? Where do you sense openness to his Spirit? What questions are people asking?

This week read and reflect daily on the scripture below. Open a natural flow of conversational prayer with the Holy Spirit as you meditate on the scriptures, inviting him to reveal himself to you. Then gather with those who journey alongside you and interact over the discipleship questions.

John 5:16-23

So the Jewish leaders began harassing Jesus for breaking the Sabbath rules. 17 But Jesus replied, "My Father is always working, and so am I."

18 So the Jewish leaders tried all the harder to find a way to kill him. For he not only broke the Sabbath, he called God his Father, thereby making himself equal with God.

19 So Jesus explained, "I tell you the truth, the Son can do nothing by himself. He does only what he sees the Father doing. Whatever the Father does, the Son also does. 20 For the Father loves the Son and shows him everything he is doing. In fact, the Father will show him how to do even greater works than healing this man. Then you will truly be astonished. 21 For just as the Father gives life to those he raises from the dead, so the Son gives life to anyone he wants. 22 In addition, the Father judges no one. Instead, he has given the Son absolute authority to judge, 23 so that everyone will honor the Son, just as they honor the Father. Anyone who does not honor the Son is certainly not honoring the Father who sent him.

Luke 19:1-7

Jesus entered Jericho and made his way through the town. 2 There was a man there named Zacchaeus. He was the chief tax collector in the region, and he had become very rich. 3 He tried to get a look at Jesus, but he was too short to see over the crowd. 4 So he ran ahead and climbed a sycamore-fig tree beside the road, for Jesus was going to pass that way.

5 When Jesus came by, he looked up at Zacchaeus and called him by name. "Zacchaeus!" he said. "Quick, come down! I must be a guest in your home today."

6 Zacchaeus quickly climbed down and took Jesus to his house in great excitement and joy. 7 But the people were displeased. "He has gone to be the guest of a notorious sinner," they grumbled.

Partner with the Holy Spirit

 Discipleship questions:

- **God is at work everywhere—but where are you currently most sensing his presence and work?**

- **What are some of the different ways God communicates that he's at work somewhere?**

- **What are some of the signs of openness we can see in people?**

- **What are some of the ways we can engage with those who are searching for God?**

- **Where do you sense God working right now?**

expression through art

Create a painting or drawing that represents to you how you see God at work in the world.

Action step questions:

- In light of our discussion, what do you hear God asking of you?

- How will you obey his prompting?

- When will you do it?

- Who will help you?

- With whom will you share what you have learned before we meet again?

III. Checking what you're hearing with scripture and your Kingdom community

Key question: What do you need to check with scripture and your community?

It's possible we might think we hear God telling us to jump off a bridge. That's why we need to check what we're hearing with scripture and also with our Kingdom community. We don't always hear accurately. If we think we are hearing something that doesn't align with scripture, it's not from God. Don't forget to check what you are hearing against the Word of God, where we know God is speaking.

One thing we also forget on a regular basis is that we need other people. We might remember at breakfast, then forget again by 9:00am. We keep thinking we should be able to do everything on our own, and this stubborn belief certainly extends to what we are hearing from God. When we believe we are hearing something from God, after checking scripture, then the next step is to see if other people are hearing the same thing. Does it line up with what others are hearing? Do others have a perspective on what we're hearing that could be helpful to us? When God is truly at work, he most often orchestrates things so we are not alone in responding to him. We need other people.

This week read and reflect daily on the scripture below. Open a natural flow of conversational prayer with the Holy Spirit as you meditate on the scriptures, inviting him to reveal himself to you. Then gather with those who journey alongside you and interact over the discipleship questions.

Acts 17:10-12

> *As soon as it was night, the believers sent Paul and Silas away to Berea. On arriving there, they went to the Jewish synagogue. 11 Now the Berean Jews were of more noble character than those in Thessalonica, for they received the message with great eagerness and examined the Scriptures every day to see if what Paul said was true. 12 Many of them believed, as did also a number of prominent Greek women and many Greek men. (NIV)*

Acts 6:1-7

> *But as the believers rapidly multiplied, there were rumblings of discontent. The Greek-speaking believers complained about the Hebrew-speaking believers, saying that their widows were being discriminated against in the daily distribution of food. 2 So the Twelve called a meeting of all the believers. They said, "We apostles should spend our time teaching the word of God, not running a food program. 3 And so, brothers, select seven men who are well respected and are full of the Spirit and wisdom. We will give them this responsibility. 4 Then we apostles can spend our time in prayer and teaching the word."*

5 Everyone liked this idea, and they chose the following: Stephen (a man full of faith and the Holy Spirit), Philip, Procorus, Nicanor, Timon, Parmenas, and Nicolas of Antioch (an earlier convert to the Jewish faith). 6 These seven were presented to the apostles, who prayed for them as they laid their hands on them.

7 So God's message continued to spread. The number of believers greatly increased in Jerusalem, and many of the Jewish priests were converted, too.

Partner with the Holy Spirit

 Discipleship questions:

- **How do you know when you are hearing from God?**

- **What kinds of "checks" do you perform to see if you are hearing correctly?**

- **Who do you regularly talk with about what you're hearing from God?**

- **How do you use scripture to help you make decisions?**

- **Tell about a time when what you heard from God did not seem to have the backing of your community. How did you navigate that?**

ask three

Ask three people you trust to give you honest, open feedback about what you are hearing from God. Try not to become defensive: just listen. Ask follow up questions as necessary.

Action step questions:

- In light of our discussion, what do you hear God asking of you?

- How will you obey his prompting?

- When will you do it?

- Who will help you?

- With whom will you share what you have learned before we meet again?

IV. Risking action in steps of faith and service

Key question: How are you stepping forward in faith?

The true test of faith is action: the meat is in the street. Hearing from God matters not at all if we are unwilling to take steps based on what we are hearing. Just as knowledge without putting it to use is void, so is hearing from God and ignoring what he is telling us.

Admittedly, this is easier said than done. There is almost always some element of risk in our obedience, and that risk can range all to the way from martyrdom to looking like a fool. Yet faith can often be spelled R-I-S-K.

> "The kingdom is about doing just as much as teaching. If you aren't doing the works of the kingdom the message isn't complete. I pray the Vineyard never stops taking the risks of the Kingdom."
>
> – **John Wimber**

from the vineyard

The question is this: What is more important to us... obeying what we are hearing from God or our own self-interests? Our answer to this question is not theoretical; it is borne out in our actions.

This week read and reflect daily on the scripture below. Open a natural flow of conversational prayer with the Holy Spirit as you meditate on the scriptures, inviting him to reveal himself to you. Then gather with those who journey alongside you and interact over the discipleship questions.

Matthew 9:35-38

> *Jesus traveled through all the towns and villages of that area, teaching in the synagogues and announcing the Good News about the Kingdom. And he healed every kind of disease and illness. 36 When he saw the crowds, he had compassion on them because they were confused and helpless, like sheep without a shepherd. 37 He said to his disciples, "The harvest is great, but the workers are few. 38 So pray to the Lord who is in charge of the harvest; ask him to send more workers into his fields...."*

Matthew 10:5-8

Jesus sent out the twelve apostles with these instructions: "Don't go to the Gentiles or the Samaritans, 6 but only to the people of Israel—God's lost sheep. 7 Go and announce to them that the Kingdom of Heaven is near. 8 Heal the sick, raise the dead, cure those with leprosy, and cast out demons. Give as freely as you have received!

Hebrews 11

Faith shows the reality of what we hope for; it is the evidence of things we cannot see. 2 Through their faith, the people in days of old earned a good reputation.

3 By faith we understand that the entire universe was formed at God's command, that what we now see did not come from anything that can be seen. 4 It was by faith that Abel brought a more acceptable offering to God than Cain did. Abel's offering gave evidence that he was a righteous man, and God showed his approval of his gifts. Although Abel is long dead, he still speaks to us by his example of faith.

5 It was by faith that Enoch was taken up to heaven without dying—"he disappeared, because God took him." For before he was taken up, he was known as a person who pleased God. 6 And it is impossible to please God without faith. Anyone who wants to come to him must believe that God exists and that he rewards those who sincerely seek him.

7 It was by faith that Noah built a large boat to save his family from the flood. He obeyed God, who warned him about things that had never happened before. By his faith Noah condemned the rest of the world, and he received the righteousness that comes by faith.

8 It was by faith that Abraham obeyed when God called him to leave home and go to another land that God would give him as his inheritance. He went without knowing where he was going. 9 And even when he reached the land God promised him, he lived there by faith—for he was like a foreigner, living in tents. And so did Isaac and Jacob, who inherited the same promise. 10 Abraham was confidently looking forward to a city with eternal foundations, a city designed and built by God.

11 It was by faith that even Sarah was able to have a child, though she was barren and was too old. She believed that God would keep his promise. 12 And so a whole nation came from this one man who was as good as dead — a nation with so many people that, like the stars in the sky and the sand on the seashore, there is no way to count them.

13 All these people died still believing what God had promised them. They did not receive what was promised, but they saw it all from a distance and welcomed it. They agreed that they were foreigners and nomads here on earth.

Partner with the Holy Spirit

14 Obviously people who say such things are looking forward to a country they can call their own. 15 If they had longed for the country they came from, they could have gone back. 16 But they were looking for a better place, a heavenly homeland. That is why God is not ashamed to be called their God, for he has prepared a city for them.

17 It was by faith that Abraham offered Isaac as a sacrifice when God was testing him. Abraham, who had received God's promises, was ready to sacrifice his only son, Isaac, 18 even though God had told him, "Isaac is the son through whom your descendants will be counted." 19 Abraham reasoned that if Isaac died, God was able to bring him back to life again. And in a sense, Abraham did receive his son back from the dead.

20 It was by faith that Isaac promised blessings for the future to his sons, Jacob and Esau.

21 It was by faith that Jacob, when he was old and dying, blessed each of Joseph's sons and bowed in worship as he leaned on his staff.

22 It was by faith that Joseph, when he was about to die, said confidently that the people of Israel would leave Egypt. He even commanded them to take his bones with them when they left.

23 It was by faith that Moses' parents hid him for three months when he was born. They saw that God had given them an unusual child, and they were not afraid to disobey the king's command.

24 It was by faith that Moses, when he grew up, refused to be called the son of Pharaoh's daughter. 25 He chose to share the oppression of God's people instead of enjoying the fleeting pleasures of sin. 26 He thought it was better to suffer for the sake of Christ than to own the treasures of Egypt, for he was looking ahead to his great reward. 27 It was by faith that Moses left the land of Egypt, not fearing the king's anger. He kept right on going because he kept his eyes on the one who is invisible. 28 It was by faith that Moses commanded the people of Israel to keep the Passover and to sprinkle blood on the doorposts so that the angel of death would not kill their firstborn sons.

29 It was by faith that the people of Israel went right through the Red Sea as though they were on dry ground. But when the Egyptians tried to follow, they were all drowned.

30 It was by faith that the people of Israel marched around Jericho for seven days, and the walls came crashing down.

31 It was by faith that Rahab the prostitute was not destroyed with the people in her city who refused to obey God. For she had given a friendly welcome to the spies.

32 How much more do I need to say? It would take too long to recount the stories of the faith of Gideon, Barak, Samson, Jephthah, David, Samuel, and all the prophets. 33 By faith these people overthrew kingdoms, ruled with justice, and received what God had promised them. They shut the mouths of lions, 34 quenched the flames of fire, and escaped death by the edge of the sword. Their weakness was turned to strength. They became strong in battle and put whole armies to flight. 35 Women received their loved ones back again from death.

But others were tortured, refusing to turn from God in order to be set free. They placed their hope in a better life after the resurrection. 36 Some were jeered at, and their backs were cut open with whips. Others were chained in prisons. 37 Some died by stoning, some were sawed in half, and others were killed with the sword. Some went about wearing skins of sheep and goats, destitute and oppressed and mistreated. 38 They were too good for this world, wandering over deserts and mountains, hiding in caves and holes in the ground.

39 All these people earned a good reputation because of their faith, yet none of them received all that God had promised. 40 For God had something better in mind for us, so that they would not reach perfection without us.

Partner with the Holy Spirit

Discipleship questions:

- **Tell about a time when you felt God was asking you to do something that made you afraid. What happened?**

- **How do you imagine the disciples felt when Jesus sent them out?**

- **How did they then go on to proclaim and demonstrate the reality of the Kingdom?**

- **What are some steps of faith that you have seen God call you or others to take?**

- **When is obedience hardest for you? When is obedience easiest?**

- **What actions do you feel God might be calling you toward? How do you feel about that?**

vineyard discipleship guides

Action step questions:

- In light of our discussion, what do you hear God asking of you?

- How will you obey his prompting?

- When will you do it?

- Who will help you?

- With whom will you share what you have learned before we meet again?

V. Discovering your giftedness and calling

Key question: How are you discovering your giftedness and falling?

from the vineyard

> "He [The Holy Spirit] releases the gifts in me, nurtures the gifts in me, and breathes on the gifts in me. If there is not a release of spiritual gifts, then I have no real authentic expression of God's heart and am lacking in kingdom fruit. The Spirit allows me to be the hands and feet of Jesus to the people that Jesus wants to touch through me."
>
> – Brenda Gatlin

One of the beauties of the Vineyard movement was summed up by John Wimber: "Everyone gets to play." Ministry is not limited to the few: it's for all of us. God wants all of us to discovery our giftedness and calling and to use those for the benefit of others.

The term "calling" has been interpreted many different ways. Many believers have spent years disengaged from ministry while waiting for a supernatural communication from God. Sometimes God gives those types of miraculous signs: the apostle Paul was practically struck by lightning and told what to do with the rest of his life. However, that's not the case for most of us. Yet that doesn't mean we don't have a calling; it just means we have a different way of finding that calling.

God has something for every believer to do in this life. We all have spiritual gifts that God expects us to exercise. We all have a contribution to make toward the coming of his Kingdom. Our task is to listen to God's voice, to live in obedience to the commands God has given all people, and to discern as we go what else God would have us do. We are to use the gifts we have and trust that God will continue to lead us. Even if we don't have a clear direction, we are still to be in motion. The basic principles of motion are that an object in motion tends to stay in motion, and an object at rest tends to stay at rest.

As we move forward in obedience to what we already know to do, more direction will be given to us by the Holy Spirit.

This week read and reflect daily on the scripture below. Open a natural flow of conversational prayer with the Holy Spirit as you meditate on the scriptures, inviting him to reveal himself to you. Then gather with those who journey alongside you and interact over the discipleship questions.

vineyard discipleship guides

from the vineyard

> "From the little boy who shared his lunch that fed over 5000 people to the woman at the well whose story impacted an entire village, to a young Jewish girl in first century Palestine who said 'yes' to God and gave birth to Jesus, we know it's true: 'everyone gets to play.'"
>
> – **Rose Swetman**

Matthew 4:18-20
One day as Jesus was walking along the shore of the Sea of Galilee, he saw two brothers—Simon, also called Peter, and Andrew—throwing a net into the water, for they fished for a living. 19 Jesus called out to them, "Come, follow me, and I will show you how to fish for people!" 20 And they left their nets at once and followed him.

Mark 5:18-20
As Jesus was getting into the boat, the man who had been demon possessed begged to go with him. 19 But Jesus said, "No, go home to your family, and tell them everything the Lord has done for you and how merciful he has been." 20 So the man started off to visit the Ten Towns of that region and began to proclaim the great things Jesus had done for him; and everyone was amazed at what he told them.

Ephesians 4:1-6
Therefore I, a prisoner for serving the Lord, beg you to lead a life worthy of your calling, for you have been called by God. 2 Always be humble and gentle. Be patient with each other, making allowance for each other's faults because of your love. 3 Make every effort to keep yourselves united in the Spirit, binding yourselves together with peace. 4 For there is one body and one Spirit, just as you have been called to one glorious hope for the future. 5 There is one Lord, one faith, one baptism, 6 and one God and Father, who is over all and in all and living through all.

Philippians 3:12-14
I don't mean to say that I have already achieved these things or that I have already reached perfection. But I press on to possess that perfection for which Christ Jesus first possessed me. 13 No, dear brothers and sisters, I have not achieved it, but I focus on this one thing: Forgetting the past and looking forward to what lies ahead, 14 I press on to reach the end of the race and receive the heavenly prize for which God, through Christ Jesus, is calling us.

1 Timothy 6:12
Fight the good fight for the true faith. Hold tightly to the eternal life to which God has called you, which you have confessed so well before many witnesses.

Partner with the Holy Spirit

 Discipleship questions:

- What spiritual gifts has God given you? How are you exercising those?

- How do you understand God's call for your life?

- What are some of the things he calls all believers to?

- How will you discern those things he is calling you specifically to?

- What practices can help you seek out God's calling in your life?

- How do God's calling and your desires fit together?

exercise

What do you already know God wants you to do? Search the scriptures for commands. Write down as many as you can.

Action step questions:

- In light of our discussion, what do you hear God asking of you?

- How will you obey his prompting?

- When will you do it?

- Who will help you?

- With whom will you share what you have learned before we meet again?

VI. Practicing spiritual disciplines in a way that increases our sensitivity and surrender to the Holy Spirit

Key question: How are you practicing the spiritual disciplines?

There are a great variety of ways to practice the spiritual disciplines. First of all, there are many different types of disciplines: prayer, meditation, solitude, celebration, study of scripture, fasting, confession, etc.

Yet even within these different types of disciplines, there are ways of practicing them that can increase our spiritual sensitivity. When we practice them by rote, doing them only because we are supposed to be doing them, we may lose sensitivity to the Spirit.

Rather, we need to approach the spiritual disciplines with an openness of the heart, led by the Holy Spirit out of a desire for God.

We can also try some disciplines we are not as familiar with; sometimes branching out into new ways of connecting with God can help us experience him more fully and in fresh ways. Talk with others to see how they practice spiritual disciplines to partner with the Holy Spirit. Read about how people from the past did as well.

exercise

Choose a spiritual discipline you are not familiar with and spend some time trying to practice it (e.g. meditation, simplicity, solitude, fasting). What did you learn through the experience?

This week read and reflect daily on the scripture below. Open a natural flow of conversational prayer with the Holy Spirit as you meditate on the scriptures, inviting him to reveal himself to you. Then gather with those who journey alongside you and interact over the discipleship questions.

vineyard discipleship guides

1 Thessalonians 5:16-22

Rejoice always, 17 pray continually, 18 give thanks in all circumstances; for this is God's will for you in Christ Jesus.
19 Do not quench the Spirit. 20 Do not treat prophecies with contempt 21 but test them all; hold on to what is good, 22 reject every kind of evil. (NIV)

Acts 17:11

Now the Berean Jews were of more noble character than those in Thessalonica, for they received the message with great eagerness and examined the Scriptures every day to see if what Paul said was true. (NIV)

Luke 10:27

He answered, "'Love the Lord your God with all your heart and with all your soul and with all your strength and with all your mind'; and, 'Love your neighbor as yourself.'" (NIV)

Hebrews 12:28-29

Therefore, since we are receiving a kingdom that cannot be shaken, let us be thankful, and so worship God acceptably with reverence and awe, 29 for our "God is a consuming fire." (NIV)

Discipleship questions:

- What has been your practice of spiritual disciplines in the past?

- How has your heart been changed through that practice?

- What would you like to see God do in your heart in the future?

- How might you branch out in your practice of the spiritual disciplines?

Action step questions:

- In light of our discussion, what do you hear God asking of you?

- How will you obey his prompting?

- When will you do it?

- Who will help you?

- With whom will you share what you have learned before we meet again?

What's next?

So you've completed this guide. What now? Is there another dimension of discipleship you need to zoom in on? If so, which one?

vineyard discipleship guides

Consider the full set of the Vineyard Discipleship Guides below and the behaviors they reflect. Where do you sense the Holy Spirit calling you to focus next?

Volume 1:

Experience and Worship God: Engage consistently with God, intentionally deepening your relationship and allowing your experience of his presence to fuel your life in the Kingdom

- Actively living out and embracing the Kingdom of God
- Seeking to know God more deeply
- Reflecting on and applying scripture in your everyday life
- Experiencing authentic, interactive dialogue with God
- Worshipping with your whole life

Partner with the Holy Spirit: Actively listening to the Holy Spirit and taking action according to what you are hearing

- Increasing ability to hear and discern God's voice
- Discerning where God is working and actively participating with him
- Checking what you're hearing with scripture and your Kingdom community
- Risking action in steps of faith and service
- Discovering your giftedness and calling
- Practicing spiritual disciplines in a way that increases our sensitivity and surrender to the Holy Spirit

Partner with the Holy Spirit

Volume 2:

Serve Sacrificially: Doing good works out of the overflow of God's love and work in our lives

- Blessing others with your words and deeds
- Partnering with others to minister in practical ways
- Ministering personally and appropriately to the poor
- Speaking up for people experiencing injustice
- Cultivating a compassionate heart as you serve others

Live Generously: Faithfully stewarding and investing what God has given you so you can contribute toward the advancement of the Kingdom

- Increasingly investing your time and resources for Kingdom purposes
- Using your spiritual gifts and abilities to bless others
- Giving your money generously and wisely
- Showing hospitality without favoritism
- Redirecting focus from self to others in line with your calling

Volume 3:

Grow and Change: Experiencing change in your attitudes and behaviors as a result of your relationship with God and others

- Pursuing God's transformation in your life and increasingly bearing the fruit of the Spirit
- Cooperating with God's healing work in your life
- Receiving prayer and processing input from others
- Living out new priorities and changed behavior
- Participating fully in a local Kingdom community

Relate in Healthy Ways: Engaging with other people in ways that reflect the heart of God toward them

- Showing respect for and acceptance of others
- Forgiving others and asking forgiveness
- Sharing biblical wisdom appropriately to encourage others
- Confronting others with humility as necessary
- Praying with and for others
- Embracing diversity in our relationships and Kingdom community

vineyard discipleship guides

Volume 4:

Make Disciples: Living in obedience to the great commission given by Jesus, which entails making more and better followers of Christ

- Deepening concern and compassionate prayer for people without Christ
- Building relationships and trust with people who are not yet followers of Jesus
- Talking about and modeling the way of Jesus
- Connecting people with a Kingdom community of discipleship
- Helping new followers make more followers

Impact Your Community: Personal involvement with others to facilitate positive change where you live and beyond

- Increasing realization that your life counts for something bigger than yourself
- Participating in God's mission in the world
- Praying for healing and reconciliation in society
- Caring for God's creation in practical ways
- Helping others cultivate healthy lives and relationships

About the Authors

Dr. Robert E. Logan has worked in full-time ministry for over thirty years as a church planter, pastor, missions leader, consultant, and ministry coach. He is internationally recognized as an authority in church planting, church growth and leadership development. Bob invests his life to equip people to be the hands, feet, and voice of Jesus to make disciples and multiply churches.

Dr. Charles R. Ridley has utilized his expertise in the area of measurement and assessment in the development of the church planter profile, which has shaped the foundation of church-planter selection all over the world. He has also done extensive work on coach competencies and assessments, conducting a qualitative international research project. A licensed psychologist and professor at Texas A&M University, Chuck earned his PhD in counseling psychology from the University of Minnesota.

About Logan Leadership

Our vision is every person living, growing and multiplying together as disciples of Jesus who demonstrate the Kingdom of God among all peoples.

Our mission is catalyzing leaders to accelerate their movement toward this vision.

Our approach integrates biblical principles with social science insights by helping leaders…

- sharpen thinking skills
- focus actions
- contextualize solutions
- create reproducible processes
- increase ministry capacity

Find out more about us at **http://loganleadership.com**.